Whirlwind

*Signs of Awakening in the
3rd Largest Unreached Nation*

*"But those who know God and obey him
will be strong and fight back"
(Daniel 11:32 NCV).*

*David Hill, Jr. with
discussion questions by Rebecca Hill*

Copyright 2012: David P. Hill, Jr.
All rights reserved

ISBN-13: 978-1461168492
ISBN-10: 146116849X

Dedicated-
To a Savior, who reached down to the depths of my sin;
To a mom, who told me that I would write a second book;
To Pastor Bill, who believed in a wayward teenager.

There is no fluff in this book! It is brief, but by no means light reading. I found myself needing to stop about halfway through to pray and repent. It contains both hope and warning. The testimonies and stories are powerful, and Scripture is the center of David Hill's source. Every Christian worker in America needs to hear this message.

Dr. Ken Read - Professor of Music/Worship
Cincinnati Christian University

'Whirlwind' is really about picking up the towel and serving the hurting in Jesus' name. I have learned that the role of a servant is to have the mindset of humility toward all people, as Christ did in the washing of the disciple's feet. Everyday God places people in your path that you have the opportunity to serve. Are you ready to pick up the towel?

Pastor Jake Jacobs – Pastor
Princeton Pike Church of God, Hamilton, OH

I found this book to be an informative and hard-hitting book. Once I began reading I did not put the book down until I had finished it. I found great hope and encouragement for the troubled times in which we live.

W. Dickson Jackson – Lead Pastor
Highway Assembly of God, Fredericksburg, VA

When more believers really believe what they say they believe, we will understand the very simple (yet not often grasped) message in this book. We will come together in unity and have impact on our cities and nation, as we will have impact and influence on the people within them! When we do this, all will understand the 'Whirlwind' David has experienced and written about.

Ford Taylor – Co-Founder of
Transformation Cincinnati/N. Kentucky

The America David Hill describes in this book does indeed resemble the backslidden Israel of Ezekiel's time. America is now a mission field in need of missionaries of every description. I thank God for people like David and Rebecca Hill, who have answered the call and are actively involved in bringing the only Hope to this or any nation: Jesus Christ. He brings new life to those broken by sin. May God send many more like-minded missionaries to our nation.

Bo Weaver – Senior Pastor
The Bridge, Wilder, Kentucky

"Whirlwind is challenging, both in that it highlights the end times and also to stop sticking ours heads in the sand and start to be the church God the Father requires for his Son. It is encouraging because when we do what we have been called to do (i.e. serve a hurting world by being the hands and feet of Jesus on planet earth), we can help impact precious lives in a massive way. This whole process is and can be both humbling and exciting. We realise that we can do all things through Christ who strengthens us."

Pastor Warren Evans – Chaplain
Bradford Bulls-Bradford, England

TABLE OF CONTENTS

1   THE WHIRLWIND OF GOD..1

2   IT IS GETTING HOTTER.....................................11

3   LORD OF THE NATIONS...........................21

4   A DIFFERENT KIND OF WHIRLWIND...........................35

5   UNCERTAIN TIMES, UNCHANGING JESUS.......................45

6   WHAT ALL THIS MEANS...59

CHAPTER ONE
THE WHIRLWIND OF GOD

"Then I looked, and behold, a whirlwind was coming out of the north, a great cloud with raging fire engulfing itself; and brightness was all around it and radiating out of its midst" (Ezekiel 1:4 NKJV).

Can you imagine being Ezekiel at the moment he sees this vision? Just an ordinary man, I am sure that Ezekiel tried to serve God in a simple way. This vision no doubt floored him. How would you feel if you were just minding your own business one day and then you started having these awesome divine visitations? Suddenly, you are overwhelmed by the presence and power of the God of heaven! There you sit speechless, as He appears in a whirlwind and a raging fire engulfing itself. I imagine any of us would feel undone at that point.

I believe that God used this experience to wake Ezekiel up to His view of reality and His love for His people. We are in need of a similar awakening in the church in America today. Ours is a fallen nation in need of the Savior's touch. It is time to get radical for Christ and experience all that He has for us. God wants to do something amazing for our nation. Rather than merely existing, He wants to show millions of Americans their divine purpose.

Ezekiel experienced an incredible revelation of God and His dealings with the nation of Israel. The brightness and glory of God appeared to him and he saw this powerful vision. So began the prophetic writings and ministry of one of the most broken-hearted men in the Bible. You see, although the Lord came to Ezekiel in such a powerful way, what He really wanted to reveal was His mercy. He is always in search of the lost and even pursues those who have turned their backs on Him.

It reminds me of Michelle: She lives in Cincinnati and through a course of events, she lost all hope. *By the end of 2010, she was hooked on crack cocaine and living on the streets. A bright and pretty young lady, Michelle had lost it all. One warm spring night she was high and suicidal. She stumbled across the main interstate through our city, Fort Washington Way. Several times she had thought about ending it all, but this time she meant it. Closing her eyes, Michelle hoped to be hit by one of the semi-trucks moving at 60 mph in front of her face!*

By some divine providence Michelle made it across the highway that night. Just hours later, she was approached by an *Urban Outreach* ministry team. Michelle was ready to surrender to the God who is always in search of those who have lost their way. As the team ministered to her and prayed for her, the leader spoke up, *"I believe God is telling me that you want to kill yourself. Can we pray for you?"* The forgiving and loving presence of Christ came right into that sidewalk gathering that night in Cincinnati.

That was the whirlwind encounter with a personal God that Michelle so greatly needed. That night she became a child of the King and was set free from addiction. Today, Michelle is a volunteer in urban ministry herself. She is living in her own apartment and working a good job. She has been totally clean and free from drugs since her dramatic encounter with Christ almost a year ago.

The Whirlwind that We All Need-

It is my earnest prayer that the book you are holding in your hand would serve as a tool for your own continued vision and revelation of Christ. He desires mercy. Just as He did in Ezekiel's day, God can visit the lost in our nation and pour out grace. He is the same God now as He was then! As He reveals His glory to us it will impart a powerful new mandate to take cities for Him. That is really what this book is all about. It is not about my ministry or calling, rather it is about each of us doing our part to win those backslidden in our nation.

My wife, Rebecca, and I minister in the inner city full-time. We often tell people that we serve on the mission field of the world's third largest unreached nation. Behind China and India, America stands as the most populous non-Christian nation on earth! Our passion is to see signs and wonders in urban America. I am not talking about the healings and miracles that accompany the preaching of the gospel either. The signs that God delights in are people saved by grace. His wonders are those who were once bound by chains of sin, but have now been freed in Christ!

Blind eyes opening and people coming out of wheelchairs should be normal for the church, but Jesus wants us to rejoice in something greater; salvation and restoration. The truth is that many in our nation have lost their faith, but now we are beginning to see signs of genuine spiritual awakening! Everywhere in urban America, powerful conversions are changing addicts into champions for Christ. I have seen it with my own eyes in the places where we have traveled to minister in churches or hold outreach campaigns. Like me, many are hungry to know if God's forgiveness can reach them at the bottom.

It seems that these last five years have been a whirlwind of sorts for my family. Through divine guidance and faith, we are finding our way in urban ministry. It is such a wild ride and can be taxing at times. Our missionary family presses on through hardship because our goal is to fulfill our mandate from God. If you are also passionate about winning America for Jesus, you will be stirred by the message of this book. We must rise up and win our nation for Jesus! He wants to use us, but we must have a fresh revelation of the majesty and mercy of God.

When Ezekiel came on the scene, Old Testament Israel was experiencing a time of great distress and upheaval. After a season of unprecedented prosperity, it was now teetering on the edge of a great spiritual abyss. War and economic chaos were stretching Israel to the breaking point. Many more issues were destroying the nation from the inside, rather than from the outside. Sound familiar? What was needed for Israel was a new revelation of divine mercy and grace. Just how deep does God's love flow for nations in such distress? I know that we need to find out in America today. Take a look around and it is easy to see that we are at the same place. Ezekiel had the difficult but privileged job of penning the thoughts and actions of God during such a time. You and I have the honor of declaring His mind and heart in a similar spiritual climate in America. Oh, we must get busy sharing grace!

It is not enough to offer a hot meal to the homeless. Church as usual is not effective in the cities of our nation. We must walk in fresh revelation and share the amazing grace of Jesus Christ. The hour that we are now living in demands nothing less than a spiritual Awakening. It is imperative that the church become alive to the presence of God again. If we are going to wake our nation up, we must be awake ourselves! We must return to our first love in the American church – there is no time to waste.

A God of Awe and Wonder-

After his first overwhelming vision of the God of glory, Ezekiel continued receiving revelation for his beloved nation. In his writings, God is depicted as a powerful and sovereign King who dwells above the cherubim. He is in the midst of the whirlwind that goes throughout the whole earth. The Lord also came to Ezekiel in a very intimate and personal way though. When God comes down and visits, there is no mistaking who He is and what He is about. He is about a real and intimate relationship with His people through Christ.

He wants to show His power, but more importantly He wants to show His grace to all who desire a real-life change. Some Americans now believe in a deistic God. This view teaches that God wound up His creation like a clock and then basically checked out of the universe. How sad that many hold to this view of their Creator, as uninterested or unconcerned with His creation. My prayer as I minister to the hurting of the inner-city is the same as my prayer for you the reader: I want you to see how close He is to you in your struggles!

As I consider Ezekiel's initial vision as it relates to our nation, I can't help but get academic for a minute. There are three definitions for the word whirlwind: *'A small rotating windstorm of limited extent. A confused rush. A violent or destructive force or agency,'* (Merriam-Webster online Dictionary).

Now I don't believe that we need a Bible college degree to figure out which of these three definitions describes the Lord's work among His people. God is certainly not a small rotating windstorm or a confused rush. Yes He does love us intensely, but He is also a God of judgment and wrath. He is a God of awe and wonder. He can be extremely 'violent and destructive' to those in opposition to His will! Ask the rulers of Jerusalem, who crucified God's Son and then refused to repent after He offered them grace upon grace through Peter and the apostles. Ask King Herod! Ask Nero, Hitler or evil dictators throughout history whom God has removed. He is to be honored above all! He raises one up and casts another down.

It seems that the American church has lost our awe of God's power. Perhaps we need to see that the whirlwind of God never changes. His grace and divine power are constant. The cross is so wonderful because the alternative is so horrible. It is time to weep over our lost sense of reverence for God in the modern American church. We come so carelessly into His presence: Hyped-up music, mass choirs and the latest technology all help us to 'get our praise on.'

Popular worship songs reinforce our self-centeredness, *"I can feel the presence of the Lord, and I'm gonna get my blessing right now!"* What about His blessing? What does God feel in our services? The God of awe and wonder is blessed by our surrendered lives. As we listen to the latest prosperity message on what is loosely called Christian television, immorality and divorce run rampant and unchecked in our churches and pulpits. We are slapping God in the face with our lifestyles and then saying, *'Praise the Lord!'*

Yes, we have a new covenant, but we have a covenant with a God who is still, *"a consuming fire"* (Hebrews 12:29). He is looking for those who will approach Him with a godly fear that causes a sense of deep respect. It is time to tremble in His presence. If we could see the terror of the Lord and understand His holiness, His grace would be that much more precious to us as believers in Christ!

God is a fire: He has never changed. However, His mercy has been revealed more fully to us in Jesus Christ. Maybe we need to remember what it was like before grace? *"You have not come to a mountain that can be touched and that is burning with fire; to darkness, gloom and storm. The sight was so terrifying that Moses said, 'I am trembling with fear.'"* (Hebrews 12:18, 21). Even the great man of God Moses was undone at the revelation of His majesty! Psalm 97 tells us that a fire goes before the Lord and destroys His enemies. He dwells in the whirlwind. We are to fear Him because of His great power. I am not talking about a terrifying fear. The fear of God drives us closer to His heart. We truly reverence Him, so we love Him.

Looking for a Clean-Cut Jesus-

Our loving Creator is also a powerful God and the Holy Spirit is actively destroying things on earth. He wrecks all that man has built, so that He can build what we really need. He is building His kingdom, filled with those of us who are surrendered to Jesus Christ. Oh yes, He is a violent rushing wind and He is cleansing His people. Jesus must be first in all things! We need this cleansing to begin in our hearts as believers, in our churches, families and then in every city in America.

What a privilege for Ezekiel to be able to see the Lord in the whirlwind and then declare His message. Jesus also wants us to see Him as He truly is today. God has given me this message for every believer… He wants to use us to reveal His glory and grace to our nation. Rebecca and I do not have a special calling or anointing because we are missionaries. The truth is that we are all missionaries to America, if we live here and believe in Jesus Christ!

There are so many perverted views of God today in America. Even in the church men twist Scripture to their own deception, making a Jesus that fits into their image. You can see it in ministers who invent a God who winks at their half-hearted worship and eventual compromise. It breaks my heart to think about pastors and ministry leaders, who are more concerned with building a big name than with reaching the harvest. Eventually, ambition gives way to pet sins.

It seems we are more focused on larger congregations and better facilities than we are on reaching the hurting. The current trend is a 'clean-cut Jesus' who does not get dirty in order to reach sinners. This Jesus is too busy helping us get a raise in order to reach our potential. In many American minds, Jesus has short hair and wears a three-piece suit. By our attitudes, we demonstrate that we think Christ hangs out with the suburban church only and drives a luxury sedan. Just like us, sometimes he feels guilty if he hears a convicting sermon and gives a hundred dollars to missions.

Do any of these realities convict us at all? If we will be honest, we all seem more concerned with our own lives than the lost. Are we truly comfortable in all of our comforts? God isn't looking for a tip for missions. He deserves the sacrifice of our lives. We must be willing to reach the lost at any cost. It is one thing to volunteer at a soup kitchen, it is quite another to give our entire lives to Christ for the broken. We had better stop looking for a clean-cut, middle class American Jesus. We must see Him as He is in reality–the King who cares for the broken and hurting.

I am not trying to pass judgment on anyone. The truth is that I look into my own heart as I share these things. Oh, to have Ezekiel's eyes and understand the glory and grace of God! If we could see eternity clearly, then we would understand the fate that awaits the sinner who does not repent. I have had enough of the false 'clean-cut Jesus.' We need the whirlwind of God to touch every house of worship in our nation, to show us His true nature.

Jesus eats with tax collectors and sinners. Like Ezekiel we must know Him, so that we can speak for Him. Our generation is responsible for our generation: The Christians on the earth today are responsible to win the lost on the earth today. We must reach them at any cost. We need the whirlwind of God to help us!

Chapter 1 Discussion Questions:

1. It is easy to look at those away from the Lord and be judgmental. But realizing that our sin is just as great can free us for ministry. Reflect on what God has saved you from.

2. We often think that we can't do God's work because of things going on in our own lives. What whirlwind is going on around you right now? How can you minister to others through it?

3. God's mercy flows during our times of distress. Describe a situation of hardship and distress in your own life.

4. Jesus Christ has placed you in a strategic mission field. Who has He placed you there to reach?

5. What can you do in your daily life (or stop doing) to make you more effective on your mission field?

CHAPTER TWO
IT IS GETTING HOTTER

"We are never more discontented with others than when we are discontented with ourselves. The consciousness of wrongdoing makes us irritable, and our heart in its cunning quarrels with that is outside it, in order that it may deafen the clamor within." -Amiel, Henri Frederic

I had to read this quote a couple times. It is powerful and true for us today in America. There is so much 'clamor' and spiritual unrest in our nation. Perhaps that is because there is so much of the same within our hearts. We are looking for some kind of escape from the 'cunning quarrels' within our hearts. Have you ever been in a situation where you just wanted relief? I can recall a rather humorous trip that Rebecca and I took several years ago…

It was our tenth anniversary in 2007 and we were excited to be driving to Disney World, the spot of our honeymoon. Rebecca was a little less excited about the vehicle we were taking; my vintage 1981 Honda Prelude convertible! It was a thing of beauty to me. Over a quarter-century old and a true antique, it had a quiet 4-cylinder engine and the original coat of faded silver paint. To Rebecca however, my dream car was a bucket of bolts with no air conditioning!

We travelled south on I-75, on our 3,000 mile 'adventure.' Things were normal enough through Kentucky and then the beautiful mountains of Tennessee. However it was August, and I began to get a little sweaty during our ride through Georgia. That was the coolest we would be for the rest of the trip! Several days later, during an afternoon run to Tampa Bay from Disney, my wife looked at me with disgust: Sweat poured off both our sun-baked faces, as we cruised down the sizzling Florida highway in my dream car.

People will act strange and do odd things when they want relief. My wife and I developed a rather interesting cooling method that day. Spray bottles from a local drug store that were filled with cold water became our comfort. We put the vent on max and sprayed these bottles in front of the hot air, while doing 70 mph down the expressway! We thus relieved ourselves for the moment with this unusual technique. I imagine that we looked pretty silly driving on the interstates of Florida and spraying ourselves off, while the top was down on our faded-silver '81 Honda. But hey, this car was a classic!

Although somewhat agitated, Rebecca and I escaped our second honeymoon with our marriage still intact. We actually had a great time together during our trip. Even though we took drastic measures to relieve our physical discomfort, spiritually we were right at home with Jesus, as He strengthened our marriage.

As funny as our vacation memory is, I have observed something similar in urban America that is not at all humorous. During these times of great global distress, people will turn to anything for spiritual and emotional relief. We see it all the time in the inner city. People, shattered by all the disappointments or pressures of life, turn to addictions for relief.

Drugs, alcohol and sexual addiction top the list of the escapes from reality. These vices always come with a high price tag though: A complete sense of hopelessness and a spiritual fever that plagues the soul. The person who seeks relief apart from Christ always enters into torment and bondage. Looking around at our nation, it is easy to see that bondage and addiction are spreading like wildfire. It has been said by atheists that, 'Heaven and hell are here on earth.' If that were really the case I would say in reply, 'Hell has gotten a lot hotter in my short lifetime!' Our world is broken and in need of God.

The heat is on as addiction spreads, crime soars and disasters become more intense and frequent. Economies are crumbling around the world and war is seemingly touching every nation. We are truly in desperate times! Our own nation is under enormous pressure. We continue to lose jobs, cope with disaster and watch leaders fall into scandals.

People are hot and irritable, searching for some form of escape. It is even a proven fact that crime rates in urban areas increase during the hottest months of the year. There is something in our human nature that causes people to become rash when we are uncomfortable. Yes, we are in a very spiritually hot time right now. We should not be surprised that it is getting worse when Psalm 9:17 says, *'The wicked shall be turned into hell, and all the nations that forget God'* (AKJV). In spite of the sufferings, it seems that the world is about to be set ablaze with a fire of a greater intensity. Hell is real and there is a terrible fate for the sinner, one that God desires for us to avoid with all of His heart.

Idolatry in God's House

"Son of man, do you see what they are doing, the great abominations that the house of Israel commits here, to make Me go far away from My sanctuary? Now turn again, you will see greater abominations" (Ezekiel 8:6 NKJV). After Ezekiel's initial vision of the whirlwind, God began to show the broken-hearted prophet even more. He was given an incredible glimpse into the supernatural realm. He began to see his nation clearly and it broke his heart, just as it broke God's heart. There was idolatry in Jerusalem, in the midst of God's own people.

Ezekiel saw the gut-wrenching sin of a backslidden nation. In this vision he was taken into the temple of God, to the very resting place of the Lord among His people. We must remember

God's passion for His house. It is to be a place of prayer for all nations. Israel had exchanged their glory for shame in the temple of the Lord. It was there that Ezekiel saw a horrifying sight…

Ezekiel saw devil-worship and foul spirits in the place of greatest consecration to God. The elders, political leaders and even the priests were worshipping idols of lust, greed and pride. They had their backs turned toward the most holy place. It was the leaders who were engaged in these perverse sins! The leaders of Israel had done the same as the people. They had all forsaken the true God. Their glory was exchanged for a lie. This is why I take sin so serious: Sin is our act of bowing before a false god. We cannot drink the cup of Christ and the cup of devils. Our hearts must cry out before His majesty, *"I am wholly yours!"*

Ezekiel lived in a time of great pressure and heart-ache. The people of God were in distress and it was spiritually hot. The ten northern tribes of Israel had been conquered – never to rise again. As Ezekiel began his prophetic writing, Jerusalem was about to be attacked and carried captive. The prophet Jeremiah had warned of final judgment and Judah was unwilling to repent. Very soon, the rest of God's people would go into exile. Ezekiel wrote his book from Babylon when his people were looking for relief.

Whenever there is trouble and people get spiritually irritable, that which is in the heart comes out. It is just like when you grab a wet sponge and put a little pressure on it, something is going to be released. God deals with people the same way: He uses hardship to show us our hearts, so that He can change them. Today, the church in America is just as broken as Israel was in Ezekiel's time. Just like then, we have set up idols in the temple. Does it stir us to pray when we realize how far we have fallen? The wedding feast is almost at hand and the bride has been committing spiritual adultery with the world. Still, God's mercy calls.

Does it break our hearts to see such a watered down and non-confrontational gospel sweep our nation? The true gospel of grace confronts, because it demands a heart change and genuine repentance. I wonder what the state of the American church looks like to Jesus? The churches where there is a powerful and life changing word preached are few and far in between. I do not speak as an uninformed critic. I share this as a concerned urban missionary to our nation, who has ministered in hundreds of churches over the last few years. The church is in grave danger today. We must see revival and renewal in the American church!

Just ask around any church foyer in America (I have been in hundreds myself). Ask people about their experience in the sanctuary. What stands out the most? Perhaps the worship band was great that morning? Maybe the pastor preached a dynamic message? What is not usually mentioned is the overwhelming presence of God. Where are the people who leave a service speechless because of the glory of God? Where is His presence?

My prayer is that people would no longer say after a service, *"What a great message! What great singing!"* God desires to hear us cry out, *"Wow, what an encounter with Jesus! I will never be the same again. What an awesome God we serve!"* I think we need to be honest about where we are at today. There is idolatry in God's house and His people are scattered and living in spiritual captivity. It is not that we have dry and empty services for no reason. We have forsaken the Fountain of Life and so our churches are mostly dead!

"For my people have done two evil things: They have abandoned me, the fountain of living water. And they have dug for themselves cracked cisterns that can hold no water at all" (Jeremiah 2:13 NLT). Like in Ezekiel's vision, today many pastors and church leaders have turned their backs on the presence of the Lord. Because of sins of lust, greed or spiritual pride, most of us no longer walk close to Jesus. Moral

failure is now rampant among pastors in every denomination. Many others are chasing all that the world has to offer. We are growing spiritually cold.

I speak from first-hand experience. Just last year, I ministered in three different churches that were rocked by scandal. In two cases, the senior pastor fell from grace just days before I arrived. All I could do was be there and bring a healing word to those left broken by the sin of their spiritual leader. And we must guard our hearts because none of us is exempt from temptation.

Even if a desire for the world is not present in ministers today, many times there is 'ministry worship.' What I am talking about is admiring what God is doing instead of admiring God! We look at our churches, our models and our ministries and say, *'that is not at all bad.'* When we feel that we have built something, we take credit away from the King and His kingdom. It is spiritual adultery to worship ministry. Oh what brokenness must enter the heart of God when His own ministers no longer love Him wholeheartedly!

The Pain of God's Heart-

Part of our calling as sold-out followers of Jesus is to shake things up and model repentance, not rock the church back to sleep. How long will it be until America becomes completely hardened and suffers irreversible judgment? Only heaven knows the answer to that question. In a violent whirlwind, God the great Judge of the earth is reaching out to us and calling us back to His heart while there is still time! Just like a natural hurricane, debris is being scattered everywhere by His wind. Consider all that is being blown around in our nation…

Church scandal after church scandal continues to surface. Just pick up a current Christian magazine and you will read about the splits, misuse of money, and worst of all the divorce among ministers. I am not trying to be a doomsday-prophet. I just want us to take an honest inventory of the church in America. It is our responsibility. Please hear me on this, dear saints: It doesn't matter what our buildings look like, how many small groups we have or how big our Christmas productions become. If we don't have the presence of God in our churches, we have absolutely nothing. It is time to hunger for God and for His presence!

Without revival we are spiritually bankrupt. How Christ's heart must ache when He says that we cause Him, *'to go far from My sanctuary!'* I am not using that scripture lightly, but with brokenness and anguish. How I need Him to keep me filled with passion, as I become His dwelling place. Instead of passion for Christ, we ministers worship our own ministries or 'secret' pet sins. Instead of the glory of His presence, many churches are content with good singing and a spirit of entertainment. I wonder if anyone reading this book feels as much pain as the Holy Spirit about these things. Do we consider that God has pain in His heart over the lukewarm church? He is the Fountain of Life, we must return to Him! God loves us and is calling our nation's churches back to Himself.

I am not trying to be 'holier than thou' either. I pray you feel the love in the words that I have written. There is no time or place for sin in the house of God. The hour is too late! Where I minister in the city, I cannot afford any spiritual games or besetting sins. People are dying every day in America because they are bound in addictions. They are about to be lost for all of eternity. I am speaking about people right next door to our churches. We must take them His presence and a life-changing grace.

Perfect Peace, Paid in Full-

As the world searches for some form of relief today, Jesus wants to make His church the sanctuary that they need. The peace that the Bible talks about is not just the absence of conflict or trouble. *"The fruit of righteousness will be peace; the effect of righteousness will be quietness and confidence forever" (Isaiah 32:17)*. This is really the message of this book. I have not written a theological paper! It is very simple: God wants fruit in our lives and it brings quietness and confidence.

In the midst of global chaos and the scandal in many churches, God offers great peace. The peace that Jesus gives can saturate every fiber of our being. It is not a peace that we can grasp with our natural mind, but one that must be embraced with our open heart. His peace is an ocean and we need to dive in today! The peace that Christ gives to a surrendered heart is called *Shalom*. That word means *'completeness, health, wholeness, welfare and tranquility.'* It is also related to the word *Shelem*, which means *'peace offering.'* Praise God! He sent His only Son from heaven to be an offering or a sacrifice to bring us peace. He paid the price for our sin in full. He brings us peace. He is our peace and complete wholeness is ours in Christ Jesus. Our great Jewish Messiah paid for our health and tranquility on Calvary's hill.

Let us receive His amazing peace in the whirlwinds that we face today. As we walk in quietness and confidence, we will give the only true relief for those in addiction. We will offer Christ as the spiritual climate gets hotter. We will refresh souls with the grace of Jesus, as they see our completeness and tranquility in Him.

Chapter 2 Discussion Questions:

1. In your life, what things have you turned to in times of stress and discomfort when you should have turned to Christ?

2. What can you begin doing or what can you remove from your life, in order to put Christ at the center of your heart?

3. Do you see Christ as the center of the mission of the church in America? Use practical examples from your church to explain your answer. How can you be a part of the solution?

4. Jesus Christ gives perfect peace to His children. Reflect on that special relationship and gift from Christ to you.

CHAPTER THREE
LORD OF THE NATIONS

"The will of God is the supreme and first cause of all things, because nothing happens but by his command or permission." – John Calvin

I am thankful for Ezekiel's prophecies. They give us a glimpse into the dealings of God with the nations and mankind collectively. You see, God wants us to understand His great plan that is unfolding in the midst of the seeming chaos in the earth today. In Ezekiel, He is seen as sovereign. He is the all-powerful Judge and King of Israel. Rest assured that God is always in control, no matter what chaos may surround – and His plans are good!

Christ is indeed King of the nations, but we need to see Him as both King and Lord. What is the difference? A king is someone who rules the land. A lord however, both rules the land and also owns the land. Jesus Christ is both King and Lord! The nations belong to Him. He rules it all and He owns it all. If God did not put up with idolatrous Israel and Judah, what makes us think that He will put up with rebellion today? It is paramount that we take heed to what He is saying to us, because all the earth is His. He has the right and authority to speak to His creation. He is Lord of the nations and Lord of our lives!

I am sometimes asked why I serve as an urban missionary. There are certainly better ways of making a living today! It is because God owns everything. He is the Creator and rightful Ruler. The drug addict, the alcoholic and the prostitute all belong to God. I serve as a missionary because He owns it all and He wants it back! The devil has taken prisoners that do not belong to him. They are enslaved to addictions and living away from God. Do we realize how much Jesus desires for sinners to be converted to Him? Christ will reach for anyone. I can recall how He changed another lost case in our city, several years ago…

James' Story-

When I met him in 2007, James was just out of jail and living on the streets. Although backslidden, he still had a very tender heart toward God. He had been raised in a good home in Cincinnati. Like me however, James found himself wandering away from Jesus Christ as a teenager. It doesn't take long to hit rock-bottom when you fall from grace! James ended up in jail for dealing drugs and then found himself homeless and in despair...

The Holy Spirit (who is so very gentle) smacked James in the head with a two-by-four named 'street-grace!' He was blown away by the atmosphere at our inner-city worship service. Former addicts and homeless people praising God with all of their hearts will make an impact on anyone I guess! God forever changed James through the passion of sinners saved by grace. Today, James no longer stays at the rescue mission…he is now the supervisor! James is a sign of awakening in the world's 3rd largest unreached nation. He is now serving with our ministry and reaches out to the hurting. James is married to a great young lady and has a wonderful family.

God desires the sinner. He desires the lost and He chases them. We have to reach more souls than ever because there is now less time than ever. The call of Ezekiel is similar to our call as believers in Christ today. He was called to minister at a crucial point in the history of Israel. After the judgments began to fall, Israel was never the same again. Ten out of the original twelve tribes were scattered and lost to history. Ezekiel's message was written to the remnant that remained.

We are told that everything written aforetime was written for our admonition. If that is the case, Christians in America had better heed the dealings of God with Israel. We are falling fast, even though today there are more churches than ever in America. After over a decade in a new millennium we now stand in the midst of a nation of backsliders, on the edge of eternity. No matter who we are or where we may live, all of the events unfolding globally point us to the fact that the 'end is near!' Christ will return in His glory to rule all of the earth very soon. It is time for the church to awaken and to hear the call of God. I pray that we respond before it is too late.

Heartbreak in our Pulpits-

As I type these words I am troubled in my soul. I am desperate without being in despair. Like David in the Bible, I am in distress for my nation and praying, *"Let us fall into the hand of the Lord, for His mercies are great"* (I Samuel 24:14 NKJV). The godly sorrow that I feel is because I just read the results from a recent survey among ministers in America…

"Less than one third of mainline clergy agree that the Bible is the inerrant word of God, both in matters of faith and in historic, geographical, and other secular matters" (Public Religion Research, Clergy Voices Survey- March 6, 2009). Wow! Can a minister even know the God of the Bible if they do not believe in the Word of God? It is foundational to all that we believe as Christians. How can we believe in Christ and be saved if we do not believe in what He says? He is the living Word - Jesus speaks to us through Scripture.

I am distressed because I heard that another pastor in my city fell from grace the other day. This man of God left his church after a moral failure. I believe that this minister (like so many others) loves God dearly. In a moment of weakness however, he fell into a trap of lust and greed. How we in the ministry must be awakened by the Spirit of God, to avoid such catastrophe!

Maybe I am so troubled because I hear of a similar new story every few weeks. Rebecca and I are heartbroken as we travel our nation. We minister in churches whose pastors have just left them in pieces. And for what you ask? Usually it is for a few minutes of pleasure or for love of the world. Perhaps I am distressed because it could be me, but for the grace of God in my life. How we must each take care to consider our own hearts and stay close to Jesus during these turbulent times.

I have preached in a pulpit where just a few weeks earlier, the pastor had announced that he was suddenly leaving. His desire was to start a new church where alcohol would be acceptable. Maybe what troubles me is that this is now commonplace across the board. God has no joy over such foolishness, displayed by those who speak for Him.

One church that I know of has an open bar and serves alcohol at some of its outreach events. I guess they feel that if they look enough like the world, they will win the world. But win them to what? I have personally listed to pastors, casually using profanity in the pulpit. Let us consider: Cursing, immorality and alcohol consumption in God's house? I am not the judge on controversial matters like alcohol, but I once heard a wise man say, *"Give beer to those who are perishing, wine to those who are in anguish"* (Proverbs 31:6).

Where are holiness and a desire for heavenly things in this hour of compromise? Good pastors, great evangelists, and even national leaders of apostolic ministries are falling on the battlefield. Many others are prisoners of their own compromise. Champions of God's grace are now becoming spectacles of Satan's wiles. I say enough! Yes, there is always mercy and restoration for these leaders, but why take the name of Jesus through the mud? Do we have no sorrow that the name of Christ is blasphemed by worldliness in the house of God? I am asking for godly sorrow. I want to share His heart and be a part of the solution.

Where are those who will weep like the prophets of old, for the heartbreak in our nation's pulpits? As I consider the whirlwind of God today maybe I am so deeply concerned because of the beggars on Christian TV. These preachers unashamedly sell the 'anointing' for the next pledge. Yes, these ministers promise prosperity and blessings to all who will 'sow a seed,' in the next 5 minutes. I say enough! Put that garbage on in the middle of the night with the other infomercials where it belongs. But for God's sake, don't call it ministry! It is no different than the money-changers whom Jesus drove out of the temple. People are dying and going to hell every day in America. We need a few preachers to get the whip out and turn over some tables in God's house!

A Different View-

I will admit that as I look at the church today, I might see things a little bit differently. Maybe it is because of my calling as an urban missionary and evangelist. Maybe it is because our mission teams constantly pull alcoholics and addicts out of the fire. Perhaps it is because I desire to be a Christ-like example to Michelle and James, who were rescued by the grace of God. It is because of these souls and the multitudes like them that I say, *'enough foolishness in the church!'* Let us preach the good news to the broken in our nation, or let us no longer call ourselves Christians!

Is that too extreme? Do we find the words of Jesus to the religious rulers of his day to be extreme? The leaders who lacked true faith in God were told, *'What sorrow awaits you, Hypocrites…you shut the door of the Kingdom of Heaven in people's faces. You won't go in yourselves, and you don't let others enter either"* (Matthew 23:12 NLT).

God wants us to pick which side of the fence that we are on in this thing! We can be religious or passionate for Christ, but we cannot be both. People are hurting and broken everywhere you go. It is time to start reaching out. The Lord tells us, throughout His Word, that a sure sign of His working will be that the hurting will receive ministry. We must share His grace with the spiritually destitute.

What does the book of Ezekiel say about ministering to these impoverished souls? We had better listen in our easy-street, recreational American society: *"As surely as I live, says the LORD God, not even your sister Sodom and her daughters did what you have done! This is the sin of your sister Sodom: She and her daughters were proud, had plenty to eat, and enjoyed peace and prosperity; but she didn't help the poor and the needy…And I turned away from them as soon as I saw it"* (Ezekiel 16:48-50 CEB).

According to this passage, God did not turn Sodom into hell because of sexual sin alone. There was a progression to their demise. Pride, lots of food, and spare time were what hardened this society against its needy. We had better read this passage carefully in the American church. Many impoverished souls are waiting for us to show concern and share Jesus! We must also realize that some of these poor souls drive a Lexus and wear a three-piece suit!

I did not write this book to make friends or tell you about your best life now. I penned these words to stir you up for the broken, even as God stirs my heart! *"God, please give us grace to reach the broken under the bridge, and also the broken CEO!"* There is no doubt that we are living in extraordinary times today. Look at the church. As I said earlier, judgment must begin with us and thank God we don't have to stay in our current state!

We need to see ourselves as the Holy Spirit does. There is a table of mercy to which we have a right to come. We serve an awesome and extraordinary God. He dwells in the midst of the whirlwind, surrounded by tempest and mystery. Yet we have access to Him and He even seeks our affections. It is time to rise up in faith and passion for America! We are called to usher in the coming of Christ and preach the gospel at the very end of time. We must by all means yield our hearts and bodies to His purpose, allowing Jesus to live through us daily.

After I wrote my first book, *The Shaking of a Nation*, I was often asked how long I thought it would be until God judged America. My response is still the same today, *"Look around, His judgment has already begun!"* The truth is that the ax has already been put to the root. The sins of the United States and the shedding of innocent blood (through abortion) have already come up before God! It is time for revival and to seek Him, that He may remember mercy in His wrath. It is not too late.

Let us listen to what Jesus is saying to us through Ezekiel's visions and His modern-day servants. They grace us with their message of a merciful, but just God! He wants repentance and a sincere new faith in Him. Yes He longs to be loved, but He is to be reverenced as well. He cares so much and He also holds our breath in His hand. Oh, His patient grace toward us!

Finding a Place of Godly Sorrow-

We believe that God is just, but does America really deserve judgment? Are we that bad? Why not just talk about grace and mercy? Certainly I believe that the cross is the center of our message and grace must be preached foremost. It is God's goodness that leads people to repentance. We must emphasize grace and mercy at all times. But we must not do it at the expense of avoiding judgment in our preaching! We must see judgment as yet another call of mercy. He disciplines us in order to bring us back to His heart.

America is under judgment. I am sorry if that offends my seeker-sensitive pastor friends! The church is under grace because of the blood of Christ, but our nation is not. God does not shed His grace on any nation but His own. He has mercy and sheds grace upon those who respond to Christ and become His people. He is still calling to America – saving those who are willing to repent. But there must be a heart-change.

In Hebrew, the idea of repentance is represented by two verbs: *shuv* (to return) and *nicham* (to feel sorrow). I can admit that I have been sorry for my sin many times. But I can probably count on one hand the times when I have really repented in great brokenness. Thank God that I made those choices, turning back to Him. To repent means that we become so aware of God's broken heart for our sin, that it causes agony in our soul. Something breaks on the inside, very deep inside. It changes our whole life in a moment and it is usually accompanied by sincere tears. The blood of Christ that washes whiter than snow is applied to such sincere hearts.

I want to live in that depth of repentance and fellowship with Christ. It is time to return to the Lord in godly sorrow. It is time to come to Christ in agony of soul, seeking change. Where is the true church that returns to the Lord in this hour of compromise? Where is our sorrow for those lost in America? Do we feel what He feels?

Since our founding, the United States has had a foundation of godly churches and leaders. A message of life and spiritual liberty has flooded our shores. How is it then that we have now shed the blood of over 50 million innocent unborn children? And we call it a political issue? Enacting national legislation and choosing to end innocent human lives (no sooner than they begin) is not a political issue. As a nation, the blood of a holocaust of unborn children is on our hands. Let us consider this very carefully: In God's eyes abortion is not a political issue. Dear friends, abortion is not even merely a moral issue. In the eyes of the Lord, abortion is the national sin of shedding innocent blood. We must see our nation as God sees it, we must pray and believe.

Dare we think that God will not avenge millions of innocent children? If we believe that then we might as well look up at heaven and say, *'You will not see or hear the cry of the innocent. You are not a just God and we will do as we please.'* I shudder at the thought, but that is what America is doing right now!

No sin will bring the wrath of God upon a nation or people group faster than shedding innocent blood. Consider God's warning to His chosen nation in the book of Jeremiah. *"And they have committed murder here, burning their young, innocent children as sacrifices to Baal. I have never even thought of telling you to do that. So watch out!"* Again the Lord warns His city, *"Jerusalem, from your mountaintop you look out over the valleys and think that you are safe. But I, the Lord, am angry, and I will punish you as you deserve" (Jeremiah 19:5-6, 21:13 CEV).*

Are We that Special?

Old Testament Israel felt they had a free pass from God. What about our beloved nation? Recently, the Lord asked me a powerful question. Whenever God speaks, it is always with overwhelming authority. He does not speak so that He can hear Himself talk, but so that we can change our way of thinking. The Holy Spirit asked me something one night not long ago: *"Why does your nation think that it is so special? Why would I judge other nations for their sin and not judge America?"*

These are very good questions! Why do we feel that we will escape if we neglect the poor and kill the innocent? Yet God still offers hope if we will turn back to Him. Whenever the Lord warns of judgment, it is so that His people will begin to pray. How can our nation turn if we will not weep for it in prayer? While America continues to call judgment down upon itself, the church continues to sleep. II Chronicles 7:14 has been used in many meetings and in many churches in America recently. But I wonder if we really grasp what it is saying? God says that He will heal a nation when His people humble themselves in prayer. Do we really believe Him? If we do then where are all the prayer meetings? How is it that the church has failed to show our great nation the way back to forgiveness and national blessing – repentance?

I believe that the richest nation on earth could learn a great lesson from one of the poorest. Haiti experienced a terrible national crisis not long ago. On January 12, 2010, a powerful earthquake struck that island nation. It resulted in nearly a quarter of a million deaths and a million homeless Haitians.

What was the collective response for this country, known for its widespread witchcraft and voodoo priests? One month to the day after this catastrophe, over a million people gathered in front of the presidential palace in Port-au-Prince. The president of Haiti had called his nation to three days of national prayer and fasting.

It appears that one of our neighboring nations believes II Chronicles 7:14: *"If my people, who are called by my name, will humble themselves, pray, search for me, and turn from their evil ways, then I will hear [their prayer] from heaven, forgive their sins, and heal their country" (GWT).* I pray that the church in America does the same before it is too late!

It is time to turn back to God as a nation. It has to start with a new faith, and new passion in the church. As we find ourselves in the spiritual gutter, we must have a fresh revelation of Christ. Yes, the Lord is coming in an awesome whirlwind to judge the nations. He is both King and Lord. But, He is also on our side! His grace reaches to the depths of our backsliding. He desires our healing! Are we willing to feel what heaven feels? Will we turn back to God in repentance?

Chapter 3 Discussion Questions:

1. Our nation is in spiritual decline right now and this always comes in progressive stages. Discuss the progression of spiritual decline in America in your lifetime.

2. How do you think God is judging America now?

3. Consider II Chronicles 7:14 and discuss it with the group. What do we need to repent of as a nation?

4. Discuss repentance. How is it different from merely being sorry for something?

CHAPTER FOUR
A DIFFERENT KIND OF WHIRLWIND

"As they were walking along and talking together, suddenly a chariot of fire and horses of fire appeared and separated the two of them, and Elijah went up to heaven in a whirlwind" (II Kings 2:11 NIV).

Talk about a great evening stroll! I cannot imagine what Elijah the prophet must have felt. It was the culmination of a difficult life and ministry. Elijah was not born at this place of ascending glory. In the life of Elijah, we see a man who was no different than we are as believers. The New Testament affirms that fact: *"Elijah was human like us" (James 5:17 GWT).*

You could say that Elijah was extraordinarily ordinary. He had a great passion for his God and his nation. We read about a broken-hearted prophet who rallies his people back to the Lord in I Kings 18. At Mount Carmel Israel had to make a decision. It was a show-down between the Lord and Baal. Nothing happened as the false prophets of Baal prayed for hours. No voice came. Elijah stood and watched the whole scene. He knew that His God was the real God. We are also sure of this concerning Christ.

The Lord answered ordinary Elijah's prayer by ending a three-year long drought in Israel. How many of us are willing to have this kind of faith for our nation? We may want to ride the whirlwind and chariot to heaven, but are we willing to take risks with our faith? That is what marked Elijah's life. He was a risk-taker for God! He knew the Lord's will and then prayed accordingly. He prayed with boldness and so can we today. If Jesus says, *"Heal the sick in My name,"* well, it is time to heal the sick. Take a risk with your faith and go out on a limb for God. He will meet you there! He always meets us when we stretch our faith.

Faith Rather than Feelings-

I must admit, I have always been amazed by the story of Elijah. Here is a prophet who literally called fire down from heaven and saw his nation begin to turn toward the Lord. You may know the story: Just a few hours later he was running for his life, pursued by Queen Jezebel. The Lord had answered by fire and the people of Israel had executed Jezebel's false-prophets at Elijah's command. She then promised to kill him for his faith. Elijah had good reason to believe that Jezebel would do it. That was her passion in life and she was good at it! Blindly zealous for her false gods and religion, she had systematically killed many of the prophets of the Lord. She had terrorized the rest that were still left in Israel.

Elijah was well aware of Jezebel's success, so he ran for his life. He then found himself battling suicidal thoughts in a cave. He forgot about his faith for a moment and gave in to his feelings. Often times these two are opposed to each other in our lives. We must learn to live by faith and not by sight. We can control our feelings based on what we know about God and His Word.

Even though Elijah faltered, he still persevered after all these things and his faith returned. Elijah ended up coming out of his self-centeredness and finished what God had called him to do in Israel: Bring a spiritual reformation. Was he a whirlwind-chariot rider? Yes! Was he a risk taker? Of course he was! But we must also remember that Elijah was just an ordinary man. He was just like us and still had to get up when he fell down.

When facing persecution himself, the apostle Paul must have learned from reading about Elijah's faith. Paul truly wanted to know Christ – even in His sufferings. That was a desire that God allowed him to live out in an incredible way. He had to allow his faith to shut down his feelings many times and had this conflict within himself. What these men of faith we read about believed, and what they felt, were diametrically opposed. That is the miracle of our faith in God! Again, we go against feelings and trust Him.

No Need to Look for Persecution-

Just like Elijah and Paul, the Lord has always called His servants to walk with Him through persecution and temptations. I have news for America though: We in the western church need not worry about being martyred for Christ. No, the devil doesn't need to persecute the American church. It seems he can keep us sidetracked with our spiritual compromise and watered-down gospel.

However, as God stirs up a true faith again it will be time to get ready for persecution in America! Let us set our faces toward God. As we return to Him with all of our hearts, hell will come at us full-force. No matter what happens, our resolve is that we will proclaim His gospel in love. Hardships cause us to draw ever closer to our wonderful Savior. In those times, we realize that He is a rock of defense in any battle and a refuge in any storm. Let Elijah serve as our example of faith and patience during the whirlwind of persecution.

Sometimes opposition can come from the most unlikely places. The truth is that many American believers are attacked by others in the church. Multitudes of believers today are struggling to find a renewed faith in these times of turmoil. Meanwhile, there is an onslaught in the church. The attack is not physical, but spiritual, from those compromised in their passion for Christ. Those who live holy and wholly for God are often criticized by those who do not. The sad fact is that many churches have become too seeker-friendly. We must be approachable to man, but not at the expense of being reproachable to God. An easy and seemingly comforting word is preached in a lot of 'successful' churches today.

Rare are the houses of worship where there is a heavenly empowered and deeply penetrating message. The need of the hour is for a gospel that causes us to cry out to God, asking for a new place of surrender and holiness. I would say that any message that does not change both the speaker and the hearer is not worth sharing. Those of us who strive for this holy ideal will find ourselves the targets of misunderstanding and even persecution. This sometimes happens in churches. We need not fear though!

It seems that many Christians today want to hear about how God will surely bless us in every area of our lives. Better jobs, bigger houses, college funds and vacations. We want our best life now! But Jesus didn't die to give us our best life now, He died to give us His best life forever! That includes all that goes with it. Yes there is great joy, but also suffering and persecution at times.

Are we willing to follow Jesus in the good times but not in the bad? We actually look forward to our best life on the other side of eternity. What a biblical idea! Until eternity, we can expect hardships with our blessing and joy. Still, Christ is faithful to comfort us in all of our afflictions. Never be discouraged saints, because our worst day with Jesus is better than our best day with the devil!

Living According to the Word?

As I travel and speak in many cities across America, I look on the church scene and see a negative trend. There is a division between those who really want to hear God and those who do not. Many are addicted to the so-called 'prophetic word,' that will give hope for better jobs, a bigger home and a happy life in this crazy world. Like little children living on junk food, our weak and feeble churches have no muscle because we crave spiritual sweets constantly. We are being flattered into a lethargic state.

While the hurting masses in our nation wait for a church to become broken in God, we frustrate the Holy Spirit with each new message of, *'Peace, peace, all is well! Go for that new job or that new car.'* One television preacher was approached by a news crew recently, *"Reverend, what do you say to your donors who sacrifice for your lavish lifestyle, private jet and multiple houses?"* His response was indicative of the attitude in many churches today: *"I am just living according to the Word!"* Ok, I have another word for you then*: "Go and sell all that you have and give to the poor!"* Let's place all our treasure in the world to come and then follow Jesus with all our hearts.

We must learn that it is not about us but it is about the cause of Christ. There are things in all of our lives that must be placed at the foot of the cross so that we can follow Him fully. We must give them to the One who can heal. Yes blessings will flow, but where is the brokenness of repentance in this hour? Where is the cry of God in the wilderness for a real heart change?

The Bible has something to say about the smooth prosperity message that goes forth by those who claim to speak for God*: "Do not listen to the words of the prophets who prophesy to you...they continually say to those who despise me, 'the Lord has said you shall have peace'"* (Jeremiah 23:16-17).

If you are tired of spiritual junk-food, then here is some meat (and potatoes) for you: You will have to enter the kingdom of God through much hardship, trials and persecution. But Jesus Christ is worth it all and He will walk though it with you! Let us really press into the genuine. We need to dive into the Word ourselves and build some spiritual muscle, not listen to a misled guide. We don't have to follow popular church trends and be blown about with every wind.

His whirlwind is inside of us and if Jesus is living there, we can follow Him! The Spirit of God in true believers today promises joy unspeakable and great peace. We can have this because we trust Christ through every trial. I for one want to be a follower of Jesus who brings unpopular biblical truth. I love Him enough to share what is really on His heart. Things are actually going to get worse before Christ returns to earth. If that divides and offends someone, then so be it!

Champions in Hiding-

Just like Elijah who hid from a queen in a cave, sometimes God's champions are in unexpected places. Remember James' story? He got married to another recipient of 'street-grace.' Randalee is also a convert from the inner-city. She is now a loving example of a godly wife. She wrote recently, *"I try to respond to anything the Lord calls me to do without hesitation because I love Him so much. This love that I have inside for Him consumes everything."* Randalee wasn't always this fired up for Christ. She was a broken and hopeless young lady when my wife met her a few years ago...

She happened to be walking by our building in the city. Randalee had been beaten down by life. Those closest to her had abused her and betrayed her trust as a child. She soon found herself trapped in a cycle of drugs and addiction, trying to numb the pain.

By the time she was a teenager she was running hard on the streets and addicted to crack. Although known as a dealer, Randalee knew that she was actually the addict too. She found herself living in the same shame of addiction that I lived in before Jesus found me in 1994. Randalee shared recently, "Drugs, crime and sex were the medications that I used to deal with the symptoms of pain, anger and shame." As a teenager, Randalee went from bed to bed and from drug to drug. She was desperate for just one more chance to dull the agony inside.

Sounds like she was pretty hopeless? Thank God He specializes in hopeless cases! In fact, those who feel they have it all together are actually far from Christ. In the gutter Jesus Christ found Randalee and saved her. She is another divine trophy of His 'street grace.' In spite of all that she had done, she found acceptance through Jesus and His servants.

Rebecca, and several other ladies who minister along-side of us, made sure that Randalee felt welcomed the day she came. It didn't matter that she was a little rough around the edges. Are any of us polished and holy when we come to Christ? No, in His eyes we are all equally filthy and in need of mercy! Randalee came in to our service that day and gave her heart to Jesus.

As I mentioned, Randalee married James and they now have a beautiful son together. She is a teen-challenge graduate and is working on her nursing degree. Randalee and James are actually reaching out to other lost souls today. They are great friends of our family and working in the city with our urban ministry today.

A Fresh Touch of Grace-

My prayer is that our nation would have a fresh touch of 'street-grace' from the church of Jesus Christ. It is time – God's future trophies and champions are everywhere. Just like He didn't give up on Michelle, James or Randalee, Christ will not give up on His lost sheep in every city. We must go out and seek them. They are at your work, in the store shopping and standing by the road asking for spare change.

To reach them we must allow God to set our hearts ablaze with His love and risk being misunderstood and persecuted. Everyone wants to ride the chariot of fire with Christ. Who among God's people is willing to suffer persecution though? Are we willing to listen to the threats of Jezebel? People are waiting to hear the truth and we must lift our voices like Elijah to reach them.

There are men and women of God on the earth right now who are waiting to be found, hiding in a cave somewhere. They are called to be champions and do great exploits for Christ. They are called to minister the gospel with authority and great power. Right now however, they are trapped in caves of sin and addictions. We must never forget that God not only cares about the ones hiding in shame, but Jesus is actively seeking them out! Will we seek them with Him?

Chapter 4 Discussion Questions:

1. Discuss a time when you were a risk-taker for God. How can you step out in new ways and take chances for Jesus?

2. Faith and feelings are often in opposition to one another. How can we keep our focus on our faith rather than emotion?

3. Have you ever had an experience like Elijah? When did you hide in a figurative cave?

CHAPTER FIVE
UNCERTAIN TIMES, UNCHANGING JESUS

"It was the best of times, it was the worst of times, it was the age of wisdom, it was the age of foolishness, it was the epoch of belief, it was the epoch of incredulity. We were all going direct to heaven, we were all going direct the other way." -Charles Dickens, A Tale of two Cities

The name Ezekiel literally means, *'God will strengthen.'* Can you put yourself into Ezekiel's shoes for a moment? It was a time of great weakness for his nation. Ezekiel was also about to experience God's heartache for His beloved Jerusalem, in a very personal way. Even though His glory was an awesome sight to behold, Ezekiel saw God as merciful and broken-hearted. The truth is that the Lord always aches for us, but we usually only notice during our times of sorrow. When we are in weakness and grief, we reach for Him. It is during those worst of times that we can discover the best of times, as we find the presence of God in a deeper way.

The outlook for the remnant of Ezekiel's nation seemed grim. Israel had sinned and suffered judgment already. The Assyrians had invaded and taken the ten northern tribes captive. They were subsequently known as the lost tribes of Israel. During Ezekiel's ministry, another prophet named Jeremiah was living in Judah. He instructed that they should submit to Babylon. Pride always thinks that it knows best and Judah's King Zedekiah would not listen to God.

From the captivity in Babylon, Ezekiel was predicting the coming collapse of Judah and the fall of Jerusalem. At the same time in Jerusalem, Jeremiah warned King Zedekiah not to rebel against the king of Babylon. The Lord still wanted to bless Judah and restore them, as He chastised them under the rule of Babylon.

But because the people would not obey God, the temple in Jerusalem was burned by the Babylonian army in 586 B.C. On that same August day, there would be another incredible heart-break in the life of Ezekiel... *"Son of man, with one blow I am about to take away from you the delight of your eyes. Yet do not lament or weep or shed any tears. Groan quietly; do not mourn for the dead" (Ezekiel 24:16, 17)*. As the Lord's heart broke over Jerusalem, Ezekiel would also lose his beloved bride. He was instructed not to mourn, as a sign to his people concerning the fall of Jerusalem.

"So I spoke to the people in the morning, and in the evening my wife died. The next morning I did as I had been commanded. Then the people asked me, "Won't you tell us what these things have to do with us? Why are you acting like this?" So I said to them, "The word of the LORD came to me: Say to the people of Israel, 'This is what the Sovereign LORD says: I am about to desecrate my sanctuary—the stronghold in which you take pride, the delight of your eyes, the object of your affection... And you will do as I have done...You will not mourn or weep but will waste away because of your sins and groan among yourselves. Ezekiel will be a sign to you; you will do just as he has done. When this happens, you will know that I am the Sovereign LORD'" (Ezekiel 24:18-14).

God will Strengthen-

"And you, son of man, on the day I take away their stronghold, their joy and glory, the delight of their eyes, their heart's desire, and their sons and daughters as well— on that day a fugitive will come to tell you the news. At that time your mouth will be opened; you will speak with him and will no longer be silent. So you will be a sign to them, and they will know that I am the LORD" (Ezekiel 24:25-27). We may think that these things seem strange and that God is dealing harshly with Ezekiel. But we have to remember that the Lord was actually broken for His people.

Through His own suffering and empathy, God would strengthen Ezekiel. Notice God's instruction to His servant, *"Yet do not lament or weep or shed any tears. Groan quietly; do not mourn for the dead."* There is a pain and a depth of sorrow that goes beyond tears. The Lord seemed like a harsh judge to His rebellious people, but nothing was further from the truth. He was beyond tears, as a faithful husband. His beloved Jerusalem had to be destroyed.

God tells the people in Babylonian captivity… *"And you will do as I have done…You will not mourn or weep but will waste away because of your sins and groan among yourselves. Ezekiel will be a sign to you; you will do just as he has done. When this happens, you will know that I am the Sovereign LORD."* He talks about groaning and even wasting away. Notice His revelation to the backslidden nation: That they would feel the same groaning and aching that He felt. He told them they would waste away because of their sin, just as it was silently tearing God's heart out. You see, through everything that God sends He reveals that His will is always restoration. Judgment is not for judgment's sake, but it is intended to lead us to restoration. Notice again that God uses the same wording, *"groan among yourselves."* There is a groaning and longing that leads to genuine repentance…

The same word *'groan'* is used earlier in the Old Testament, at a similar time of devastation for God's people: *"Whenever the LORD raised up a judge for them, he was with the judge and saved them out of the hands of their enemies as long as the judge lived; for the LORD had compassion on them as they groaned under those who oppressed and afflicted them"* (Judges 2:18). We must remember that God suffers with His people. No heart breaks (because of pain and sin) as much as His. He is always there in such times, groaning with His people. As we begin to feel this deep aching and intense yearning for God in times of distress, a new intimacy with the Lord is birthed in us.

Consider what Paul wrote to the Roman Christians: *"In the same way, the Spirit helps us in our weakness [want of strength, weakness, illness, suffering, calamity, frailty]. We do not know what we ought to pray for, but the Spirit himself intercedes for us with groans that words cannot express" (Romans 8:26).* Dear believer in Christ do you understand? It doesn't matter if your beloved Jerusalem is in ruins. Even if you have lost all that you cherish and love in life. Even if your closest loved-one were to pass away... God is still there. He is groaning with you. What comfort and assurance that should give us!

The Lord is looking for those of us who will not wait for calamity, to groan intensely for Him. Who is willing to share His broken heart and His groaning for the backslidden church? Ezekiel's heartbreak over his people is what is needed in the church in America today. We are living in a time of great moral and spiritual decay. Yet the glorious light of Christ is still here! He is aching and even groaning that we understand His love and compassion for our nation. Christian, we must speak to the remnant. Ezekiel's book was recorded as a warning to the remnant at Jerusalem, and as an encouragement to those in exile. We must realize that Ezekiel's book is for us personally as well. Like all of Scripture, it was written as an exhortation to encourage us today.

The latter part of Ezekiel is a message of the hope and future restoration of God's chosen people. Are we as believers not living in exile now? Our hearts may be fully turned to the Lord, but we are still in this sin-sick world. We are waiting for that glorious day when our God brings us into our promised land! We are not home yet, so let us stir our faith and long for heaven. The Lord encourages each of us to look beyond the worst of times, and our current suffering and groaning. We must see that Jesus is preparing a place for us in His kingdom! Just like a modern-day Ezekiel church, we must call the remnant of God to turn from sin and embrace our coming restoration. God will strengthen the hearts of those who carry such a message of hope.

Christ Speaks to Those Who Seek-

I believe that we can learn a lot from the Lord's dealings with His ancient people Israel. There are also lessons to be learned as followers of Christ, from Ezekiel's brokenness. You see, he had to be strengthened for a reason. When His precious wife died on the same day that Jerusalem was destroyed, it no doubt made him feel undone. He needed a new revelation of the Lord. When I look around on the Christian scene today, it seems that everyone wants a revelation. Do we realize what we are seeking though?

Everybody wants Christ's miracles and blessings, but nobody wants to share in His suffering. Many ministers are even deceived by this desire. Some TV preachers promise blessing and increased anointing, as you give to their ministries. I heard one fellow share that a special blessing would come when people gave $1,000!

What a terrible lie. A special blessing comes as we give whatever we have, in sacrifice. It doesn't matter if it is $10 or $10,000. When Ezekiel's revelations came, I doubt that he was seeking them. I am sure he was not selling them for a $1,000 donation to his ministry! I am convinced that those revelations caused him great weakness and distress. In his flesh he couldn't take what the Lord was saying. But God became his strength.

Jesus Christ does not speak today to those who seek the miraculous or special revelations. He speaks rather to those who seek Him with all their hearts. Let me say that again: He speaks to those who seek Him. I don't know about you, but I am willing to receive the revelation that He gives, no matter the price. Like Ezekiel, we must come to this place of hunger for God and allow

Him to break us down. He is able to make us strong again! Discovering this close intimacy with the heart of Jesus and sharing His strength is the true rest that we all really need in our souls. Our worst times can become our best times, as His Spirit delights our souls in affliction and trials.

Experiencing Eternity without God-

In America we believe that everyone is going to heaven. During these troubled times, most people have convinced themselves of a terrible deception: Everybody gets to go to heaven in the end. It doesn't matter that there isn't a burning passion for Christ, as long as there is a mental acknowledgement of Him. The Bible puts forth a powerful challenge to those believing the lie that all you must do is believe that God exists: *"You believe that there is one God. Good! Even the demons believe that – and shudder" (James 2:19).* I too believed that I was alright as a teenager. I understood who Jesus was, but that was not enough. I was not following Him.

"They will be punished with everlasting destruction and shut out from the presence of the Lord and from the majesty of his power" (II Thessalonians 1:9). When I came to Christ, it was a time of great personal distress. It was certainly the worst of times for me. I cannot fully describe my spiritual, emotional and mental state on that blessed night when Jesus rescued me…

I had wrecked my life in 1994. O.J. Simpson had just been arrested, U2 and other mid-90's bands were rocking the charts and many in my generation were caught up in a futile 'party' mentality. I followed the crowd and found myself using anything to fill the void in my soul. My friends and I lived for drugs, parties and girls – in that order. We were cold and selfish and loved only ourselves. Little did I know that on June 18, 1994, this teenage prodigal was about to split Hell wide open!

I was becoming increasingly unhappy with my life and stuck in a cycle of self-destruction. Life was a party and I was happy with all my friends, but I somehow found myself trying to escape reality through addiction. My buddies and I would get high in the bathroom at school or in the parking lot before a ballgame. We were all out of control in our thirst for another thrill.

I am so grateful for His wonderful 'street-grace' in my life! It came on that fateful warm summer night, in the suburbs of Cincinnati. I was hanging out with a few friends and some girls at a buddy's house. We were soaring on LSD, drinking heavily and stoned out of our minds. I must have consumed a toxic mixture that night, because reality began to fade fast around midnight.

Somehow I knew that God was taking my life and showing me what was just ahead for me if I continued on my downward spiral. In an instant, eternity met my pathetic reality and I felt that the Lord loved me more than I could ever fathom. I was surrounded by this love and a peace so deep that I could not understand it. At the same time however, I felt shame for the way I had lived my short 18 years. I felt the agony of Jesus' heart for my backslidden condition and how far I had fallen. God was groaning in His heart over my selfishness. I did not understand it then, but Jesus was seeking me. I want you to know that He will come looking for you in your darkest places and reveal His goodness there.

In order to comprehend what I saw next, you must realize that God has no pleasure in death and hell. Jesus came from eternity and suffered in the flesh, so that we could have heaven! He is not willing for one soul to go to hell. God hates the fact that people still choose to reject Him. Oh, it is so true… *"For I take no pleasure in the death of anyone, declares the Sovereign Lord. Repent and live!"* The *New Living Translation* is even more compelling: *"I don't want you to die, says the Sovereign Lord. Turn back and live"* (Ezekiel 18:32 NIV & NLT). That night I turned back to Him.

As my friends continued to party into the night, I was suddenly surrounded by flames. I was in torment, my conscience burning my mind and soul with my sins and misdeeds. I am not talking about a vision or a dream, but something which I experienced that was more real than anything you will ever feel on earth. The flames were not physical, but spiritual in nature and they brought more suffering than you could ever imagine.

It was spiritual pain, much greater than pain in your body or even the worst emotional suffering. It was the agony of being shut out from the presence of a holy God and being lost in your sins forever…knowing that you chose for it to be that way. As the apostle Paul said in II Thessalonians 1:9, those in hell are truly punished with, 'everlasting destruction from the presence of the Lord.' There, all those who lived self-destructive lives on earth will experience true eternal despair. At the moment that I encountered hell, I was distraught the most by the revelation of His holiness. I was also shamed by my unfulfilled earthly desires – yes, I desired sin. I was guilty and I had rejected His love.

An Intense Reality-

On that night, I left my body and experienced the next world. Everything is so much more real when you leave this earth. You see better, hear better, and you physically feel things at a totally different level. I felt things that night that are not possible to experience in your physical body. It is an intense reality. That is the reason why heaven will be so great for the believer in Jesus: It will be real – His love will be very real! And the great news is that it does not take a lot to get to heaven. Jesus paid the price! All that we must do is have a genuine and life-changing faith in who He is and in what He has accomplished for us. For those of you who serve God and are reading this, don't let my testimony put fear in you. No, rejoice because our names are written in heaven and let hell motivate you to plead the cause of Christ with sinners!

As I said, in eternity all of your senses are heightened beyond imagination, including smell. Many feel that the next life will be a dream-state. Nothing is further from the truth. Leaving earth is like waking up from the dream and being faced with the ultimate reality of eternity. If we are lost in our sins, it will be for eternity...

I can still recall the smell of death and torment from that night in 1994. It was as bad as any stench of the worst sewage on earth. As I became undone by what I was experiencing, I somehow knew deep in my heart that this was my last chance to turn back to God. I instinctively felt His grace tug at me, as He allowed me to touch eternity without a real dependence upon Him.

Half in the physical world and still caught up in the spirit realm, I left the party as fast as I could that night. I began praying under my breath and calling upon Jesus to save my soul. As I walked outside, my spiritual eyes were opened and I saw eternity unfold before me. A battle ensued, as I experienced the torment of the demonic forces around me and in me, through the drugs that I had consumed. I suffered the incredible turmoil of making the decision of whether to turn back to Christ or not. As lost as I knew I was in that moment, somehow I still loved my sin and desired it! The greatest tragedy of hell is that the people who are there will get there because of their own desires. Souls are not lost by accident, we choose to be lost. We miss heaven because we love sin and wish to remain in it. Oh, the heartache of it and the love that brings us to our senses! As my will struggled with God's, I turned and looked and suddenly I saw that I was leaving my body at an incredible rate of speed.

The Whirlwind of Hell's Gates-

Just ahead, I saw a powerful whirlwind and vortex of what I can only describe as a massive spiritual-sewage drain. I knew this spot well because it was near a local shopping mall. What I saw in the spirit realm however, was much different than the natural landmarks that I had recognized before that night. I was looking at a massive vortex and a gateway to eternity.

The spirit world exists alongside the natural. There is a realm of angels and demons that influences our natural realm and vice-versa. Every decision we make and sincere prayer that we pray to Jesus affects this realm. Our faith can move mountains in this realm and spiritual forces are moved by our worship of God or neglect of Him. As I saw the next world, demons and lost souls were being sucked into this powerful whirlwind vortex or 'gateway' by the multitudes. It was similar to what you would imagine with the incredible force of a 'tractor beam,' from science fiction movies. For me and the rest of the lost souls and demons, there was no escape. There was nothing to hold onto and no other place where we could go.

I was drawn by a force greater than my own will or possible strength. If I would have been the world's strongest man, my efforts of resistance could not have begun to compare with the power that pulled me closer to eternity without Christ. I am not sure I understand everything that happened to me that summer night, but I do know that I was brought to the literal gates of Hell. These gates are not some wrought-iron fence with a pitch-forked devil standing by them. I was pulled to hell's gates by a force and spiritual darkness that you cannot imagine. I had no power to escape them either. It was like going down into a powerfully swirling vortex, with no way out.

Those who enter hell are gripped by two things at once: The total horror and the complete inescapability of it. There is no way for a lost soul to escape the torment of hell when he dies. When a sinner passes away without Christ, their soul is pulled into hell like a spiritual magnet. There is no other option, no purgatory and no rest for them. The gates that I saw on that summer night were a constant and powerful pulling 'whirlwind.' The best way to describe hell's gates is that they are alive, in a sense. I personally believe that there are a lot of these gates in existence on earth today. Although we can only get into heaven one way (through a living faith in Jesus), there are many ways, bondages and addictions that will take the sinner to hell.

The gates drew me into a vortex of suffering. Nobody had to tell me that I was about to enter hell. As I said before, reality takes on a whole new meaning and you know things instinctively in the next world. The loneliness and hopelessness that I felt in that moment cannot be compared to anything else. It is a place of constant suffering. Although I saw other souls and demons, I was alone. Those who choose to reject Christ are truly 'lost' forever.

As I was pulled by the gates and the demons that I had surrendered control of my life over to, I again began to pray. In a panic I called on Christ. "I love you Jesus," my heart cried out. I now realized that I didn't want hell, but a new relationship with God. Something in the depths of my soul told me that I was not created for this awful reality. I begged Him to come back into my life. For a reason I will never understand, I was given another chance and God heard my prayer. Suddenly, as if jarred awake from a nightmare by an unseen force, I was back in my body. I began to walk back to my house, still reeling from my experience and encounter with eternity.

I never made it home that night and was arrested by the Hamilton County Sheriff's Department. Having just seen hell and in a drug-induced panic, I resisted arrest and was charged with assaulting a police officer. Through my experience I have come to believe that hell is literally in the heart of the earth. There, the devil and his angels will be joined by the multitudes of those who have rejected Christ. Flames, suffering and gross darkness await all who fight against God. It is so very real.

Motivated by Eternity-

How we must preach the gospel and take grace to the streets while there is time! Every soul must hear. Those under a bridge and those in the tallest office building must understand the message, by our love. Everlasting destruction and eternal pain are awaiting the sinner who dies in their sin. But heaven calls, oh how it calls!

As I think about my experience, Michelle's whirlwind testimony, and the story of James and Randalee, I cannot help but imagine something: Where would I be today, save for the grace of God? I can safely say that I would already be in hell! By our testimonies, we all had one thing in common: We realized where we were going and what we deserved, but then we did something. Motivated by His love and eternal grace, we called upon Jesus. That is all that is necessary to escape hell and have a new life in Christ – just simply calling upon His name!

How the heart of God breaks for all of the souls who choose sin and self instead of grace and mercy. The cross of Christ forever paid our sin debt and we have a great reason to rejoice as Christians. Eternity motivates us to believe and live the message.

We must fix our hearts on heaven and be thankful. Heaven is so wonderful because hell is so horrible. God is so good to allow us to have an eternity of peace and joy, rather than what we deserve. In spite of how much the unrepentant sinner will suffer, I believe that we Christians have had it wrong for decades. The motivation in many soul–winning efforts and crusades has been the lost state of mankind. While this matters immensely, there is a much greater motivation for sharing Christ…

As much agony as I experienced on the night that I tasted hell, there was a greater pain. During the entire experience, I was aware of how much sorrow I had caused the Lord. You see friend, the real tragedy of hell is that God's heart is broken for those people who reject Him. Although there will be no sorrow in heaven, Jesus will forever bear the scars that paid the price for *all* of mankind's redemption. He will eternally be known as the Lamb of God. The motivation in reaching the lost in our world is not, *'How will the sinner feel on the judgment day?'* We must ultimately consider what the sinner's fate will cause God to feel!

Still, we the redeemed will enjoy peace and joy forever. Heaven is even more real than hell and it must be our focus. If we are motivated by eternity, we will keep heaven in view at all times. We must be mindful of what awaits the sinner, but we must not focus on the darkness. We are to set our minds on things above and use our imagination to consider the greatness of God's glory.

During the worst of times, people are open to Christ on a whole new level. There is no doubt that our world today is ripe for harvest. There are people at your job, in your neighborhood and even in your family who are ready to listen. They feel that they are already in hell. Their lives are so filled with pain, confusion and despair. We do not need to persuade some people about hell, many feel that they are living in it already.

In these worst of times, God can give us His strength like He did for Ezekiel. Even when we lose that which is most precious to us, His grace is enough. We are His remnant and we have a message. Multitudes in our nation's cities are lost. Are we willing to be motivated by eternity and show them heaven through our lives? They were created for nothing less than His presence!

Chapter 5 Discussion Questions:

1. Who can you reach out to that should be part of 'God's remnant,' but is currently living as one of the 'lost tribes?'

2. Have you ever experienced a sorrow and 'groaning,' that brought you closer to Jesus? Have you considered that He shares your heartache and pain?

3. *Leaving earth is like waking up from the dream and being faced with the ultimate reality of eternity.*' This statement goes against everything in our culture! How much do you agree with it? Please explain your view.

4. In what ways can you understand the realities of heaven and hell personally?

CHAPTER SIX
WHAT ALL THIS MEANS

"And there shall be signs in the sun, and in the moon, and in the stars; and upon the earth distress of nations, with perplexity; the sea and the waves roaring" (Luke 21:25 KJV).

Just like when Jesus gave this message regarding the last days, there is an end coming. He spoke of dramatic events that would impact the whole earth. If something happens in the sun, moon and stars, the whole earth will be affected. Jesus' words imply global tribulation and they are for us today. There has never been a time like we are living in now. There are signs and perplexity, the sea of nations is roaring in unrest and turmoil.

So what is the point of all of these things? Why was this book written and why were the stories of 'street-grace' shared? The fact is that we are now living in a Psalm Chapter 2 moment. The King is set on His throne and the nations are raging! Psalm 2 exhorts us to submit to the Son. That is the first point. We must give our all to the One who gave His all for us! It is time to rise up with new passion for Christ because of the urgency of the hour in which we live.

Everyone is searching for an answer in these difficult times. The earth is staggering because of mankind's collective rebellion against God. If we could see into the spirit-realm, we would see debris everywhere. His whirlwind is removing everything that can be shaken. But if you are living for Jesus Christ, you are a part of a stable kingdom that cannot be shaken! That is what I wanted to encourage you with through this book. Those who sell out for Jesus in this hour will not only survive, we will thrive! We will do great exploits for God because we know and trust Him. We will fight back against the wiles of the devil.

The devil is taking no prisoners. He is making new disciples each day. People are becoming addicted to drugs, alcohol, sex and a host of other sins. Others are addicted to television, recreation or even their jobs. Good church folks are sometimes addicted to religion or church activity. If the enemy cannot get us idle, then He will try to get us too busy. He does not want us to hear God. Let us walk in balance, receiving grace and then giving it away daily. Let us learn to be still before Him.

No, the enemy is not pulling punches right now. It is time to rise up and fight! We have a just cause and we have an awesome God. If we truly know Him, we will fight back and rescue the prisoner. He can turn our nation back to Himself, if we only believe. Where is this kind of faith in America? Where are those who know God and are strong, ready to fight? Even though Satan is raging, many of us are rising up with passion and faith. Many leaders are falling into sin, but we must become strong in righteousness. We must fight for our cities!

It is time to heed the call of *Isaiah 52: "Wake up, wake up, O Zion! Clothe yourself with strength. Put on your beautiful clothes, O holy city of Jerusalem, for unclean and godless people will enter your gates no longer" (NLT)*. We are living in a day when God will no longer tolerate compromise in His house. Soon, there will be no place for those who walk in compromise and live halfway for God. We will live in a glorious New Jerusalem, where no sin may enter. We must wake up and live holy, so that by grace, we receive this blessed hope!

Getting Busy in the Worst Times-

God is in control right now, but the fact remains that this is also the worst of times. The headlines in the newspapers and the anchors on our networks daily and dutifully declare the chaos of the hour. Brothers and sisters in Christ, we don't have to look far to see the pervasive hopeless spirit in the earth. It is enough to bring the strongest of us to our knees.

Governments have no answer. Global economic chaos continues. And wars and rumors of wars are affecting or threatening every nation. In many parts of the world, evil dictators and rogue nations threaten peace with nuclear capability. Nations are seeking to acquire powerful weapons in a sickened play for domination and power. Wave after wave of cataclysmic natural and man-made disaster continues to flood every corner of the globe.

But there is also a beautiful picture! There is a master plan being worked out in front of our very eyes. For those of us who believe and love God, it is a good plan. Why have we reflected on the writings of an ancient prophet? How can that possibly relate to the job we have today in revealing 'street-grace' to the lost? The fact of the matter is that we are the closest generation to ever live to the coming of Christ. That should shoot spiritual adrenaline into our very souls!

The King is coming! The first time that Jesus came, He was born in a manger. He came to live as our example for holiness and to die as our substitute for sin. The next time that Christ comes it will be as the Lion of Judah! The apostle John tells us of a conquering King on a white horse: *"His eyes are like blazing fire, and on his head are many crowns. He has a name written on him that no one knows but he himself" (Revelation 19:12).*

He is coming in a whirlwind to judge the earth and establish His eternal kingdom. Even now the effects of His judgment are being seen. He is coming as a triumphant King, to rule and reign! And those who believe will be by His side. It seems like the waves of the nations are roaring out of control, but He has orchestrated everything. Our success as Christians is His chief aim. You see, God is not bent on our failure, but on our becoming champions for Christ. The cross and the upper room both proved that. He wants us to win!

All of this means that we must not be moved away from our hope! It is time to get busy for God in the worst of times. Dear believer in Christ, we must press on because our victory is near. I am not pretending to have answered all of the questions about why we face such a bleak national and global forecast. What I do know is that Jesus predicted all of these things and He is not moved. We should not be moved either.

With all the confidence in me I can assure everyone reading this book that the Lord is in complete control! The truth is that He is seated on His throne, always in a position of rest. We should be at rest too. The peace of God should saturate our hearts, as we realize that Jesus is praying for us continually. There is never a moment that He is not interceding on our behalf (Hebrews 7:25).

It may be the worst of times, but God can turn it into the best, as we follow Him closer. Rather than sit around and complain that the sky is falling, it is time to get busy for Christ. The more we entrench ourselves in the cause of Jesus, the more souls we will reach for Him. It does not matter to God if you are a street preacher, a businessman, a housewife or suburban pastor. There are so many hurting people everywhere right now. It is time to start sharing His mercy and grace in a greater way. You are an ambassador for God's kingdom in a dark world.

To Those Who Have Yet to Believe-

The Lord has a plan and a course of action that He is taking during these times. His plan is actually the reason that we see such an acceleration of events. Like a great cosmic Puppet-Master, Jesus Christ is pulling all of the strings! Everything happens because He commands it or He allows it.

Through it all, God is working for the good of those of us who love Him. The bad news is that things will not be alright for you in the end, if you refuse to hear Him speaking. If you do not yet know Christ in a personal way, He is groaning and aching for you. He wants you to see that He loves you more than anything!

If you have received nothing else from this book, let this remain with you: In the current global chaos, God wants you to experience His peace. There has been a cosmic war between good and evil since Adam and Eve's fall from grace. At stake is the eternal destiny of mankind. God wants you on His side in this epic battle. Christ has already won the war for us at Calvary!

He proved His love to you for all time and eternity, when He paid for your sin. All you have to do is call on Him today, but you must do it with all of your heart! He is awesome in power and coming in a great whirlwind – coming to your rescue, as you call on Him. I will not pretend that you can pray a little prayer and shake a preacher's hand and everything will turn out alright. I do not hold to the theology that a prayer alone or water baptism can make your life acceptable to God. No, we must respond fully to the finished work of the cross.

There must be a total faith and an utter dependence upon God. Along with your confession of sin, there must be a genuine brokenness. Along with our calling on Jesus, there must be a new love for Him. That is God's desire, a total and complete change! Jesus is King and Lord and He is in charge of everything. He will give you peace today, but only as you surrender to His will.

How can a loving and compassionate God be in control when so much heartbreak is taking place? That is simple, just open the Bible and read: *"I form the light and create darkness, I make peace and create calamity; I, the Lord, do all these things" (Isaiah 45:7).* Yes, God is in control of evil and He permits it for a reason. He does not do wrong, but He will allow wrong in His sovereignty. The Lord uses each circumstance and experience to teach important lessons. He is more concerned with our eternal destiny than our current comfort or even our feelings.

I found out a long time ago that He is willing to see me greatly offended, in order to get my heart right with Him! He won't pull any punches in His passion for our salvation and holiness. He is calling to you today, through the pain that you feel. Jesus is always honest about our spiritual condition. He is so concerned that He will order everything to the end that we may know Him. Think of the power that He has to control all things, and do it for our eternal welfare. We must hear Him speaking to us in the whirlwinds that we face today!

As I said earlier, it seems that things are certainly getting spiritually hotter today in America and in many nations. Multitudes are acting out of shear agitation and are no longer in control of their lives. It is during these times of intense suffering and global distress that we can find perfect peace. His quietness and confidence are available to us today, as we walk with Jesus.

It is Time to Fight Back-

"Do you see what all these things mean? All these pioneers who blazed the way, all these veterans cheering us on? It means we'd better get on with it. Start running—and never quit! Keep your eyes on Jesus, who both began and finished this race we're in... And now he's there, in the place of honor, right alongside God. When you find yourselves flagging in your faith, go over that story again, item by item, that long litany of hostility he plowed through. That will shoot adrenaline into your souls" (Hebrews 12:1-3 The Message).

How we need some new spiritual energy, how we need adrenaline in our souls! Ezekiel and Elijah were no different than we are today. We too can experience the whirlwind of God in our walk with Christ. Whether God is tearing things down or He is catching us up like Elijah, Jesus is still the same. His desire is a real relationship and sweet communion with all of mankind.

This message must never be compromised: He is a God who is just, but also passionate about reaching those who are about to enter hell. A revelation of hell should give us a passion to save souls. How will Jesus feel on that day if we do not reach them? We must be concerned and broken for the lost, but more concerned for God's heart. How He feels and the passion of His heart is the most important thing. The Lamb of God deserves to receive what He paid for – the souls of men.

Dear saints, Christ is both King and Lord, and we must give an account to Him. I am praying especially for ministers in this hour, that we would fall in love with Jesus all over again. With so many deceived and not even believing in the Bible as the Word of God, we need a revival among ministers today! It is time to get a fresh revelation of Christ as we seek God. There is no room for a compromising message. We cannot be so focused on gathering a larger crowd, that we neglect to tell that crowd that it costs everything to follow Jesus. It is time to fall totally in love with Christ and the souls He came to save. God wants those of us in leadership to end the foolishness. It is time to pursue God with all of our heart. Those we lead are counting on it!

I pray that every believer reading this book would have a fresh boldness in the light of coming persecution. God always gives us strength, whether attacks come from church members, government leaders or even our own families. It is time to be like Elijah on Mt. Carmel and stand for Christ in the face of intense opposition. We may find that persecution comes from our natural families or even those who claim to be our brothers and sisters in the Lord. No matter what we face, God will help us. Let us esteem our relationship with Christ above all else! Rebecca and I are asking for new patience and love in the face of persecution.

Standing in the Whirlwind-

Can you imagine being Ezekiel at the moment he saw the whirlwind of God? What about Elijah, as He was caught up in a whirlwind to experience heaven? Just ordinary men, I am sure that they tried to serve God in simplicity. Let us have this same heart and stand for Christ in the whirlwinds of life. We must remember that He groans and intercedes with us. As we do this, a new revelation of Christ and His grace will manifest in our lives.

It may be that you are praying one day or singing in church and the God of glory appears to you. You may be privileged to see Jesus in a raging cloud of fire engulfing itself. I do know that He is coming to take home those who love His appearing!

Pray for Michelle, ask God to keep her in the palm of His hand and protect her from temptations. Remember James and Randalee, who are serving the Lord and preparing to be used in a greater way. Pray that they will press on and move into all that God has for them. Consider the hurting and the addicted in your own city. How can you walk a mile with them and share Christ?

Even if you do not feel called to urban ministry, hurting and addicted people are all around. Trust me, it does not matter where you live, they are there. It might be that teenage boy living next door, desperate to break free from addictions. If the Lord can change me, a hell-bent teenager, then He can change your heart and even your entire city. I don't pretend to believe that everyone reading this book is called to urban ministry. If you know Jesus though, you are called to reach souls. Ask God to lead you to the ones who are broken and groaning, living on the edge of eternity.

You never know if that lady begging for spare change (or the one sitting in the office next to you) is suicidal. God can and will break the chains of hopelessness, no matter what the surroundings. God is doing His work of 'street-grace.' He meets people on the street, right where they live. He rescues those who are in the gutter. He gives us opportunities to reach out to them every day.

As we consider God's whirlwind, we can walk in the same brokenness as Ezekiel. We must feel His compassion for the lost. We must continue to pray for our leaders. Most importantly, we must have godly sorrow for the missing presence of Christ in our churches. If we allow God to break us, we will see an awakening. This will come only as we earnestly call on the Lord. He is waiting for us to feel His burden and groan after His presence.

Rebecca and I pray that this book has served as a tool for a new personal revelation of Christ. I hope that you have a new boldness in evangelism since reading it. He is the same yesterday, today and forever. He is able to visit America again and pour out grace. It is not too late to see spiritual awakening come to the third largest unreached nation. As we stir our faith and passion for Jesus, it is not too late for America!

Chapter 6 Discussion Questions:

1. How do you see the earth staggering and the nations raging in these last days?

2. Do you believe we are in the last days before the return of Christ? Why or why not?

3. How can you be an "ambassador for God's kingdom in the world?"

4. Who is God calling you to walk a mile with? Where is He calling you to reach out to others for Christ?

5. What do you need to do to fall completely in love with Christ?

My Whirlwind Evangelism Commitment:

With God's help, I commit…

-To search out opportunities for evangelism.

-To find the lost and walk two miles with them.

-To serve those in need of a Savior.

-To be more concerned with the reality of eternity than with the reality of today.

-To help bring home the prodigal.

-To be the hands and feet of Jesus not in word only, but in my daily life.

With the example of Jesus, the power of God and the leading of the Holy Spirit, I commit my life to winning the lost!

_____   _____
Signature   Date

www.shakingofanation.org
(visit for more information, blogs & teaching materials)

*All Scripture quotes are taken from the NIV, except where noted.

*Testimonies in this book are true and all individuals described therein are real. Permission has been obtained from these persons to use their names and stories.

Made in the USA
Charleston, SC
06 March 2013